X 3   8/09

DISCARD

THE AMERICAN FLAG

Author: Kelli L. Hicks

Rourke
Publishing LLC
Vero Beach, Florida 32964

www.rourkepublishing.com

PHOTO CREDITS: © George Clerk: Square Frame; © Eliza Snow: Oval Frame; © Joe Gough, © Mark Tenniswood: page 5; © Library of Congress: page 6, 12, 13, 14, 15; © Simon Spoon: page 7, 8; © ulia taranik: page 8; © Jan Tyler: page 9; © Terraxplorer: page 10; © Wikipedia.com: page 17; © Chase-Statler, Washington (Library of Congress): page 18; © Keith Muratori: page 19; © Master Sgt Mark A. Suban, USAF: page 20; © Gordon Galbraith: page 21; © Dan Thornberg: page 22; © U.S. Air Force photo by Lois Walsh, Brandon Laufenberg: page 23; © Jonathan Brizendine: page 24; © Michael Martin: page 25; © Diane Garcia: page 26; © Igor Karon: page 28; © U.S. Airforce: page 29; © christine balderas: page 30.

Editor: Jeanne Sturm

Cover design by: Nicola Stratford, bdpublishing.com
Interior design by: Heather Botto

Library of Congress Cataloging-in-Publication Data

Hicks, Kelli L.
 The American flag / Kelli L. Hicks.
    p. cm. -- (American symbols and landmarks)
  ISBN 978-1-60472-343-4
 1. Flags--United States--Juvenile literature. I. Title.
 CR113.H53 2009
 929.9'20973--dc22

                        2008014136

Printed in the USA

CG/CG

Rourke Publishing

www.rourkepublishing.com – rourke@rourkepublishing.com
Post Office Box 3328, Vero Beach, FL 32964

Table of Contents

A Symbol for Our Country

When you think of the United States, what pictures do you see? Maybe you think of the Statue of Liberty or a bald eagle soaring through the sky. Our country has many symbols.

A **symbol** is an object or idea that holds special meaning to a place or to a group of people. The American flag is an important symbol to the people of the United States. It is a symbol that stands for independence and freedom.

You can see the flag flying proudly on government buildings and schools, and sometimes in front of your neighbor's house.

5

Revolutionary War

Have you ever wondered about where the idea for our flag started? We have to look far back in history to find the answer to that question.

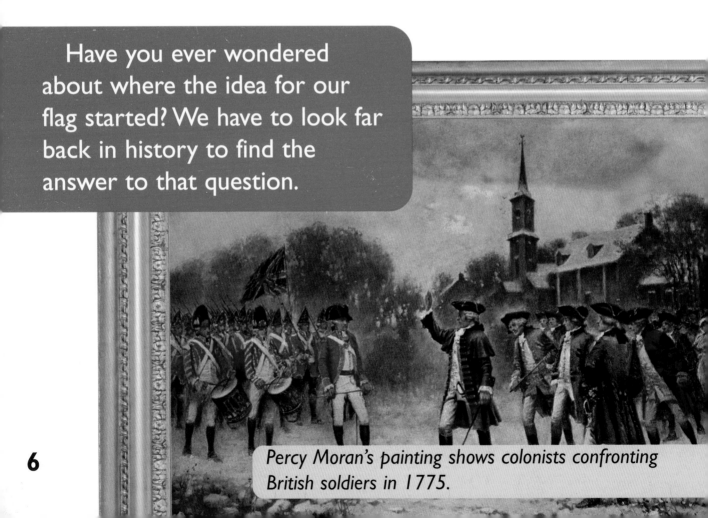

Percy Moran's painting shows colonists confronting British soldiers in 1775.

Many early settlers came to America from England. As time went by, the colonists became more **autonomous**. They established the new land and were thriving in it, but England still had control of the government.

Colonists began to feel that England treated them unfairly. England required high taxes from the colonists for items like tea and paper, but the colonists didn't have a voice in how the colonies were ruled.

Members of the Sons of Liberty are shown harassing a tax collector.

As the colonists became angrier, they began to prepare for war. Different groups and different colonies made flags to show support for the cause and to display their desire for freedom from unfair government. American ships flew a flag with a liberty tree on it with the words, *An Appeal to Heaven.* The Continental Navy used a flag with a snake over red and white stripes that stated, *Don't Tread on Me.*

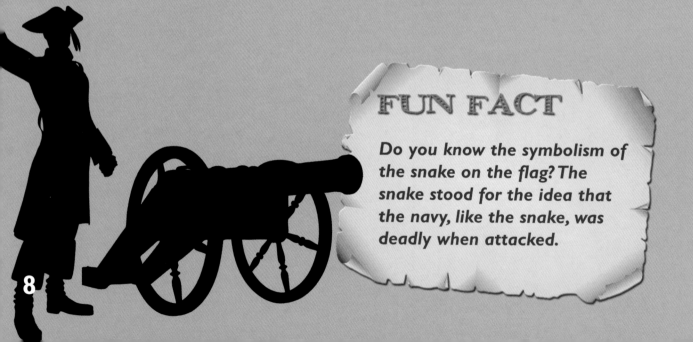

FUN FACT

Do you know the symbolism of the snake on the flag? The snake stood for the idea that the navy, like the snake, was deadly when attacked.

DONT TREAD ON ME

9

Once the war had progressed for two years, the Continental Congress decided to establish an official flag to represent the **unity** of the new nation.

On June 14, 1777, Congress passed the First Flag Act. It stated that the national flag of the United States should be made of thirteen alternating red and white stripes and thirteen stars, one star and one stripe to represent each state of the union. They suggested placing white stars on a blue background to represent a new **constellation**.

Although not originally chosen for their meaning by the Continental Congress, the colors represent different ideals. Red stands for valor, white for purity, and blue for perseverance and justice.

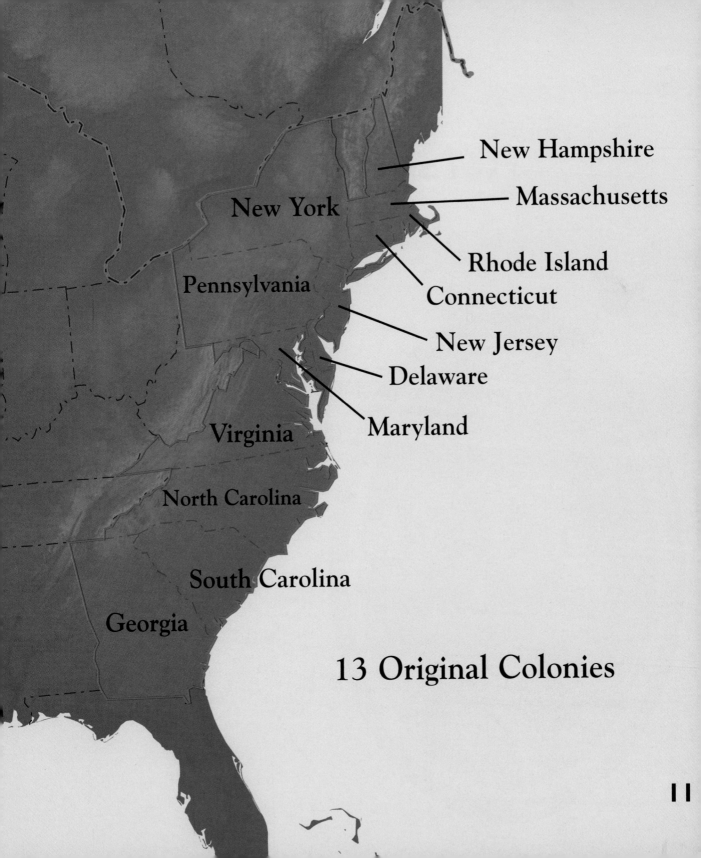

New Hampshire

Massachusetts

New York

Rhode Island

Connecticut

Pennsylvania

New Jersey

Delaware

Maryland

Virginia

North Carolina

South Carolina

Georgia

13 Original Colonies

Betsy Ross

Who was Betsy Ross?

Elizabeth Griscom Ross (1752-1836) was a seamstress who lived in Philadelphia. Betsy often embroidered shirts and mended clothing for George Washington.

G. Liebscher honored Betsy Ross by painting a portrait of Betsy at work.

12

Betsy told her grandson that George Washington came to her with some other members of the Continental Congress in 1776. The group asked her to sew a flag based on the design they brought her.

Unfortunately, there is no record of a meeting taking place, and the Continental Congress did not chose the stars and stripes design until 1777. No one knows for sure who designed or sewed the first flag, but all agree it has become an important symbol for the unity and freedom of all who fly it.

FUN FACT

Francis Hopkinson (1737-1791) was a signer of the Declaration of Independence, and some historians wonder if he designed the first flag. He sent a bill to the Continental Congress asking for payment for his flag design. He never did get paid!

The Star Spangled Banner

In 1812, The United States was again at war with England. There were many battles on land and sea. One particular night in 1814, the British attacked Fort McHenry with a variety of colorful bombs and explosives trying to take over the city of Baltimore.

A lawyer named Francis Scott Key (1780-1843) watched the battle from a ship in the harbor. As the bombs exploded, Francis watched to see if the flag continued to fly throughout the battle.

FUN FACT

It wasn't until March 4, 1931, that President Herbert Hoover, depicted in this photograph from 1929, signed a law to make the Star Spangled Banner our national anthem.

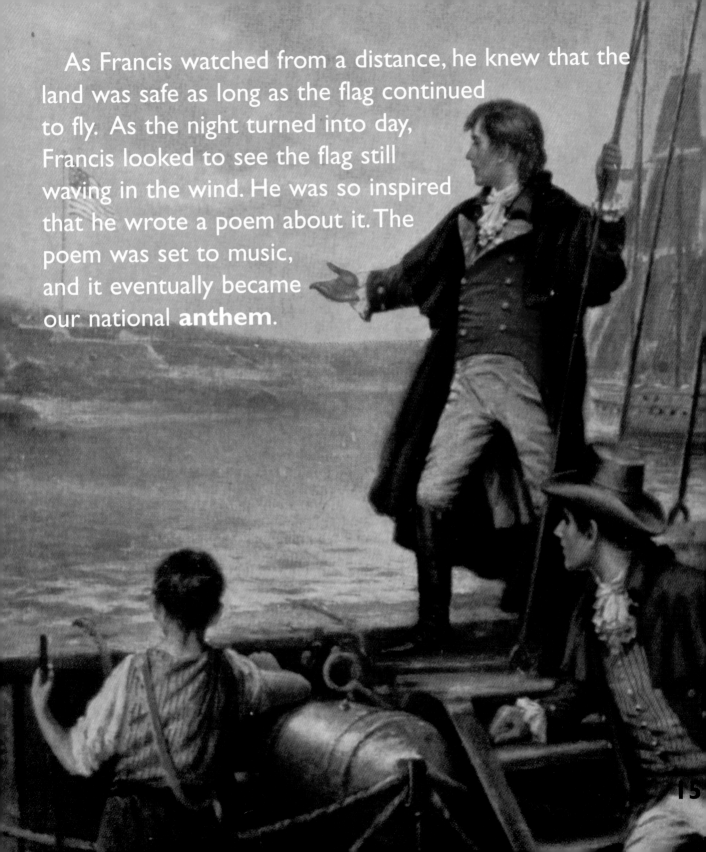

As Francis watched from a distance, he knew that the land was safe as long as the flag continued to fly. As the night turned into day, Francis looked to see the flag still waving in the wind. He was so inspired that he wrote a poem about it. The poem was set to music, and it eventually became our national **anthem**.

Old Glory

Have you ever heard someone call the flag Old Glory? A shipmaster named Captain William Driver (1803-1886) came up with the name in 1831. Captain Driver went on many voyages on his boat, the *Charles Doggett*. On one mission, he helped to rescue some sailors who mutinied on the ship *The Bounty*.

Some of his friends gave him a flag with twenty-four stars on it. As he saw it wave for the first time, he exclaimed, "Old Glory"! During the Civil War, rebels wanted to steal the flag and destroy it, but it was never found. Over time, even as people retold the story and the flag design changed, the phrase *Old Glory* remained. The Smithsonian Institute now keeps Captain Driver's flag.

Partial Historical Progression of Flag Designs

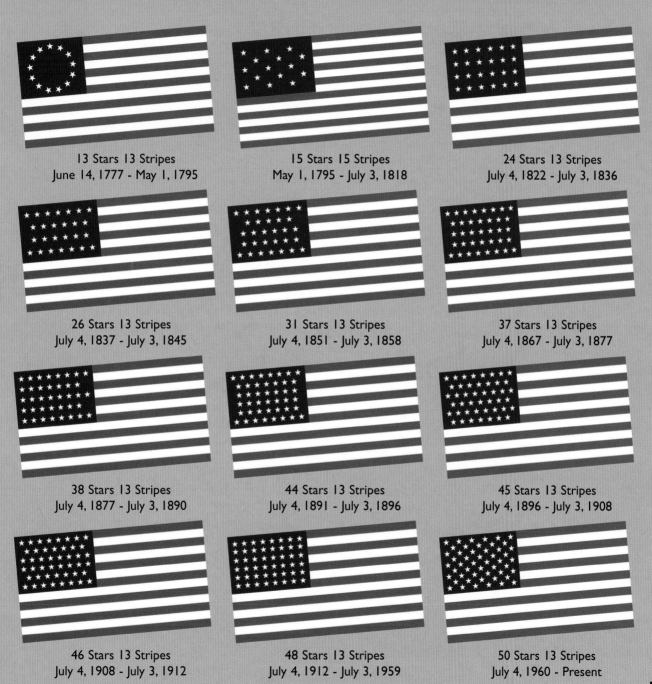

13 Stars 13 Stripes
June 14, 1777 - May 1, 1795

15 Stars 15 Stripes
May 1, 1795 - July 3, 1818

24 Stars 13 Stripes
July 4, 1822 - July 3, 1836

26 Stars 13 Stripes
July 4, 1837 - July 3, 1845

31 Stars 13 Stripes
July 4, 1851 - July 3, 1858

37 Stars 13 Stripes
July 4, 1867 - July 3, 1877

38 Stars 13 Stripes
July 4, 1877 - July 3, 1890

44 Stars 13 Stripes
July 4, 1891 - July 3, 1896

45 Stars 13 Stripes
July 4, 1896 - July 3, 1908

46 Stars 13 Stripes
July 4, 1908 - July 3, 1912

48 Stars 13 Stripes
July 4, 1912 - July 3, 1959

50 Stars 13 Stripes
July 4, 1960 - Present

National Flag Day

The Fourth of July is a special day to **commemorate** the birth of our nation. People celebrate their independence with gatherings, parades, and fireworks. Did you know that the flag also has a birthday? Flag Day originated with school children who decided to celebrate the creation of our national flag. Historians believe that students in Wisconsin had the first celebration in 1885.

Harry Truman signs the papers to make Flag Day a national holiday.

A few years later, in 1889, a school in New York planned a ceremony to celebrate the birthday of the flag as well. Over time, the celebrations spread to other schools and states. In 1949, President Harry S. Truman recognized Flag Day on June 14 as a national holiday.

The Pledge

A **pledge** is a promise or an oath that shows respect and loyalty. In 1892, readers saw the original Pledge of Allegiance published in a children's magazine. The author, Francis Bellamy (1855-1931), wrote the pledge in honor of Christopher Columbus and his voyage to America 400 years earlier.

Citizens often recite the Pledge of Allegiance at public gatherings, government functions, community events, and even in schools.

When saying the pledge, you should place your right hand over your heart and face the flag. You should salute the flag in a standing position.

21

Showing Respect

There is a code that tells people the **etiquette**, or the proper ways to show respect to the flag. The flag always flies in an upright position, unless it is necessary to fly it upside down as a distress signal.

The flag should never touch the ground. It is disrespectful to wear the flag as clothing. However, the police, firefighters, and even scout groups may wear a patch that shows the flag.

There are also rules on how to properly display the flag. When displaying the flag outdoors on the same flagpole as another flag, the American flag should always be at the top. Also, when displayed with other flags, the other flags can be smaller but never larger than the American flag. The United States flag should always be the first one raised and the last lowered. Unless it is waterproof, the flag does not fly in bad weather.

The American flag should always be folded properly.

Times of Mourning

We can show respect to the victims of a tragedy or honor the death of an important person by flying the flag at half-staff. On September 11, 2001, an attack on the World Trade Center in New York City caused the deaths of more than three thousand people. The flag flew at **half-staff**, or half-mast, to honor the lives that were lost.

To fly the flag at half-staff, first the flag is raised to the top of the flagpole, and then lowered to a position half way between the top and the bottom.

Memorial Day is another occasion where we fly the flag at half-staff to honor the men and women who lost their lives defending the freedom of our country.

The Current Flag

How did the flag change from the original thirteen to fifty stars? As each new state joined the union, the flag received an additional star.

The current American flag has fifty stars and thirteen stripes. The fifty stars are white and represent the fifty states. The stars are arranged in rows. There are five rows that have six stars alternating with four rows that have five stars. The flag has thirteen stripes to represent the original colonies that fought the British for independence.

Timeline

- 1775 ~ The Revolutionary War begins

- 1776 ~ Betsy Ross claims she sewed the first American flag.

- 1777 ~ The Continental Congress passes the First Flag Act to adopt an official national flag with thirteen stars and thirteen alternating red and white stripes

- 1812 ~ America declares war with England

- 1814 ~ Franics Scott Key writes the Star Spangled Banner

- 1869 ~ The post office releases the first postage stamp that displays the American flag

- 1892 ~ The Pledge of Allegiance appears in a youth magazine

- 1897 ~ The United States adopts a law to protect the flag from desecration

- 1931 ~ Presedent Herbert Hoover adopts the Star Spangled Banner as our national anthem

- 1942 ~ Adoption of the national flag code to provide rules for displaying the flag

- 1949 ~ President Truman approves Flag Day

Glossary

anthem (AN-thum): a religious or national song, often sung by a choir

autonomous (aw-TON-uh-muhs): self governing or independent

commemorate (kuh-MEM-uh-rate): do something special to honor or remember an event in the life of an important person

constellation (kon-stuh-LAY-shun): a group of stars that forms a shape or pattern

etiquette (ET-uh-ket): rules of polite behavior

half-staff (HAF-STAF): the position halfway between the top and bottom of a flagpole or mast

pledge (PLEJ): to make a sincere promise

symbol (SIM-buhl): a design or an object that represents something else

unity (YOO-ni-tee): a whole or totality as combining all parts into one

Further Reading

Firestone, Mary. *Our American Flag*. Coughlin Publishing, 2006.

Landau, Elaine. *The American Flag*. Scholastic Library Publishing, 2008.

Thompson, Sarah. *American Flag Q&A*. Harper Collins Publishers, 2008.

Websites

www.bensguide.gpo.gov/3-5/symbols/flag.html

www.usa-flag-site.org/history.shtml

www.foundingfathers.info/american-flag/

Index

About the Author

Kelli Hicks is an educational consultant with over fourteen years of teaching and administrative experience. As a charter member of the Tampa Bay Area Writing Project, Kelli works to share her love of reading and writing with both teachers and students. She currently lives in Tampa, Florida.